THE STORY OF NOAH'S ARK

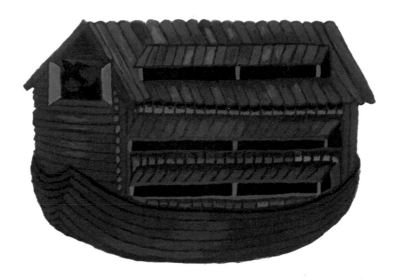

Library of Congress Cataloging in Publication Data
Emhardt, Erna.
Noah's ark.

Translation of: Arche Noah.
Summary: God directs Noah, the only good man left on
earth, to build an ark, so that his family and two of
each species of animal may be saved when the great
flood comes to destroy every other living thing.
1. Noah's ark – Juvenile literature. [1. Noah's ark.
2. Bible stories – O. T.] I. Haubensak-Tellenbach,
Margrit. II. Bible. O. T. Genesis VI, 5-XI, 17. III. Title.
BS658.E6313 1983   222′.1109505   83-1894
ISBN: 0-517-55050-4

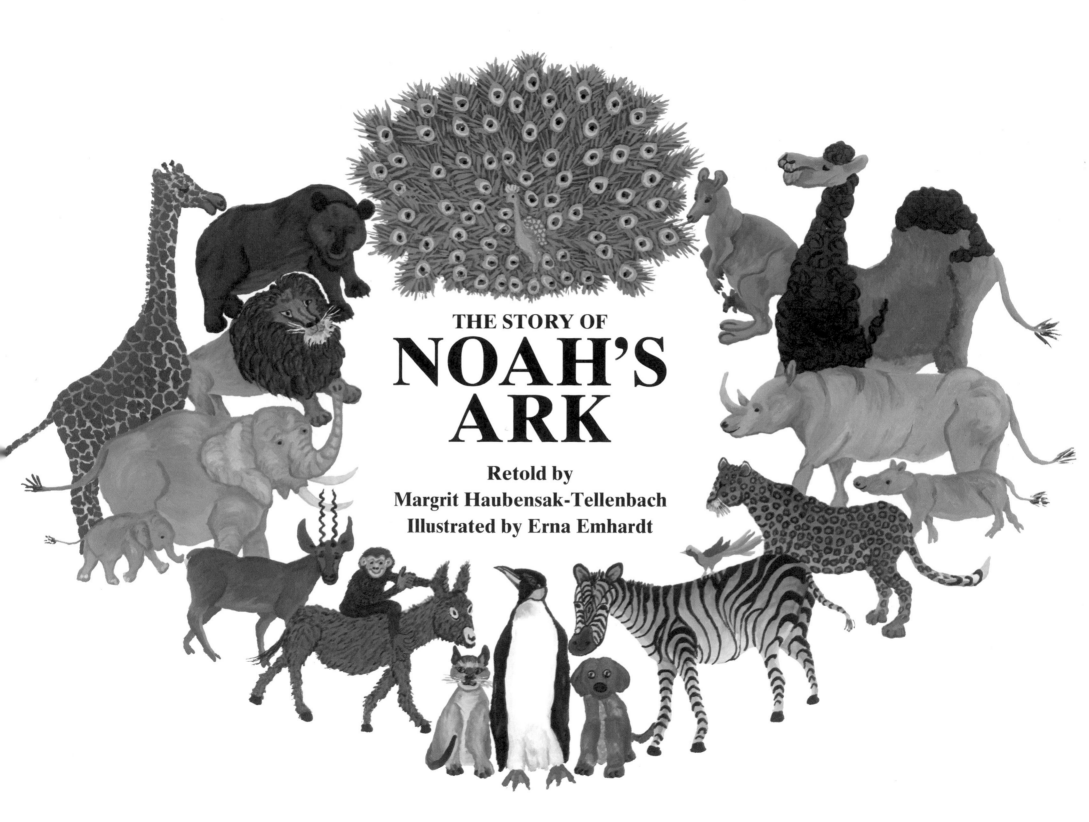

THE STORY OF
NOAH'S
ARK

Retold by
Margrit Haubensak-Tellenbach
Illustrated by Erna Emhardt

CROWN PUBLISHERS, INC., NEW YORK

4   Many, many years ago a man named Noah lived with his wife, Namah, and their three sons, Shem, Ham, and Japheth. Shem had brown hair, Ham had black hair, and Japheth had blond hair. Each of them had a beautiful wife.

Many, many years before Noah's time, God had created the world and all the people and all the animals. He had created all the flowers, trees, and plants; all the mountains, rivers, and valleys; all the seas, seashells, and sands; all the skies, winds, and clouds; all that existed. He had made the sun, the moon, and the stars. Everything. And He had been pleased.

But then the people became evil; they were selfish and violent and did not behave as God wished. God was angry and spoke to Noah, who alone, He thought, was good.

"The people are so bad," He said. "I wish I hadn't made them. I want to destroy them. I want to destroy the earth and everything that lives on it."

Noah was frightened to hear God talk that way. But God went on, and Noah listened. "I am going to send a flood," He said, "and I am going to let the whole world drown. You, your wife, your sons, and their wives I will spare. And two of each animal, one male, one female."

"But … how are we to be saved?" asked Noah.

God replied, "Take some gopher wood, it is like pinewood, and build a big boat, an ark. When the ark is finished, take your family and each pair of animals on board. Remember to take food for your family and fodder for the animals. You will all be safe in the ark when the flood comes."

So Noah took his sons to the woods to cut down gopher trees. They worked long and hard with axes and saws to chop down the many trees that would be needed to build the ark.

6   When Noah and his sons began to build the ark, they were careful to make it just the way God had instructed. The ark had to be three hundred cubits long, fifty cubits wide, and thirty cubits tall. There were to be three floors, a huge door in the middle of one side, and a window measuring one cubit all the way on top. All the cracks were to be sealed with pitch to keep out the waters of the coming flood.

As Noah and his sons worked on the ark, many people gathered to watch. They wanted to know what Noah and his sons were building.

"I am building an ark," said Noah, and he told the people about God's anger and about the coming flood. He asked them to be good in the hope that God would change his mind.

But the people did not believe the flood would come. They laughed at Noah and his sons for building a boat on dry land nowhere near water.

Noah did not say anything. He kept on building the ark, and the people continued to make fun of him.

8   At last, the ark was finished. Noah, his wife, and his sons carried the food for the animals and the people into the ark.

The animals came to the ark on their own. Noah did not have to call them or to go get them. Two by two, a male and a female, they walked into the ark.

The big animals lived on the bottom floor. The cattle, the horses, the donkeys, the elephants, the camels, and the zebras all lived there together with the lions, the panthers, the tigers, the lynxes, the bears, and the bulls. The rabbits, the foxes, the woodchucks, the monkeys, the deer, the wild boars, and the llamas all lived on the bottom floor, too.

The birds were on the second floor. There were blackbirds and sparrows, parrots and peacocks. There were ducks, geese, cuckoos, and robins, storks, ostriches, owls, and seagulls, eagles, doves, ravens, and puffins.

Noah lived on the top floor with his wife and his sons with their wives. The smallest animals lived there too. Worms, glowworms, mosquitos, and beetles, lizards, ants, gnats, and butterflies were all happy together. Bees, moths, spiders, and fleas all settled in on this floor.

After each person and each animal had found a place, Noah looked one last time at the people who were standing near the ark and who had laughed and made fun of them. Then he closed the doors. It would have been very dark now if a giant pearl had not been hanging in the middle of the ark. The pearl shone brightly and gave all the creatures light.

12   After Noah, his family, and the animals had spent seven days aboard the ark, it started to rain. It rained and rained, as it had never rained before. The rain crashed down from the sky like one huge, foaming waterfall.

The people cried and screamed and banged on the ark. "Let us in!" they yelled. But it was too late. The great flood covered everything. Gardens, fields, forests, houses, and hills all disappeared under the water. The water climbed higher and higher until even the tallest mountain was completely covered. Every living creature that was not in the ark had to drown.

The ark rocked back and forth on a wild sea. Inside, everyone fell all over one another. The animals screamed and shrieked and roared and squeaked in their terrible fright. Even Noah and his family were alarmed.

It rained for forty days and forty nights without stopping.

Then the rain stopped.

The ark floated quietly on the water. Noah, his wife, his sons, and their wives continued their chores, which included feeding the animals. Feeding the animals was hard work because there were so many of them. And now there were even more mouths to feed because some of the animals had given birth.

16 Slowly the water began to seep into the ground, and one day the ark stood still. It had landed on Mount Ararat. After forty days had passed, Noah opened the window and let a raven fly out. The raven was happy that he could finally fly freely again.

"*Caw! Caw! Caw!*" he crowed in amazement and joy, spread his wings way out, and tore through the air. "I'm going to pick out a fat worm or a fat caterpillar. Maybe I'll even catch a mouse. That'll be a treat!"

But the raven did not find a worm or a caterpillar or a mouse. The whole earth was still covered with water. When the raven saw that there was nothing below him but water – no trees, no bushes, no grass, just the tips of the highest mountains peeking out of the water – he thought, "I'll fly back and forth over the water and make lots of wind with my wings so that the water will dry quicker." And the raven continued to fly back and forth.

18   Later, Noah let a dove fly out to see if the waters had dried up yet. The dove was as white as snow and she, too, was happy to be able to fly freely again.

"I will look for a beautiful tree and build a nest there," the dove thought and she started to look for a beautiful tree. But all the trees were still covered by water. The dove flew and flew. She saw nothing but water and another snow white dove, but that was herself mirrored in the water. So the dove went back to Noah in the ark because there was nowhere she could stay, nowhere she could build a nest.

20   Noah waited seven more days and then let the snow white dove fly out again. In the evening she came back with an olive branch in her beak. There was a lot of excitement in the ark – and a lot of happiness – because now everyone knew that the water had gone down and the land had reappeared. How else could the dove have brought back an olive branch? She had to have broken it off an olive tree no longer covered by water!

"Let us out of here," the animals said to Noah. "Let us out of here. We are tired of being in the ark."

"We would like to climb up a palm tree and swing around," said the monkeys.

"We would like to dig deep tunnels in the earth," said the moles.

"We would like to bark at the moon," said the dogs.

"We would like to kiss the flowers," said the butterflies.

"We would like to lie in the sun again," said the cats.

The cows wanted to eat fresh grass, the bees wanted to gather honey, the polar bears longed for the ice, and the lizards for a wall with lots of cracks. The tigers longed for the jungle, and the ostriches wanted sand in which they could poke their heads.

But Noah said, "Patience, patience. We must wait another seven days."

After these seven days had passed, Noah let the snow white dove fly out for the third time. This time she did not come back. She had found the olive tree again from which she had broken the branch. The dove stayed there and built a nest.

And then God spoke to Noah. "Now go out, all of you, and live on the land again. Go and have lots of children." And they all went out into the open air and felt much happiness and freedom.

24   Noah, his wife, Namah, Shem, Ham, Japheth, and their wives, and all the animals had lived in the ark for exactly one year. The world they saw now was new again and clean and beautiful.

When God saw how happy they all were, he said, "I will never again destroy all the people and animals. I will never again send a flood. I promise you that."

And He put a rainbow in the clouds and said, "This is a sign of my promise. Every time you see a rainbow, you will remember my promise."

And that's how it was many, many years ago.

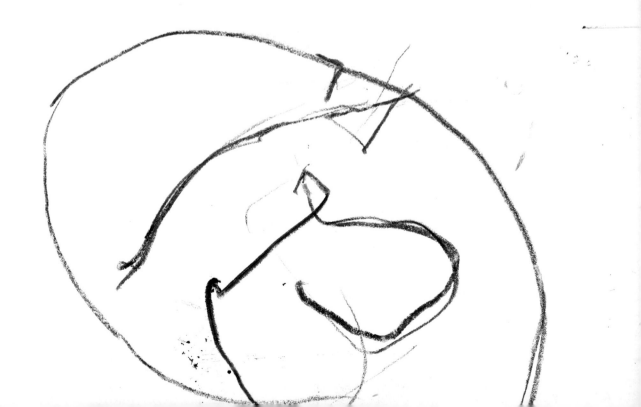

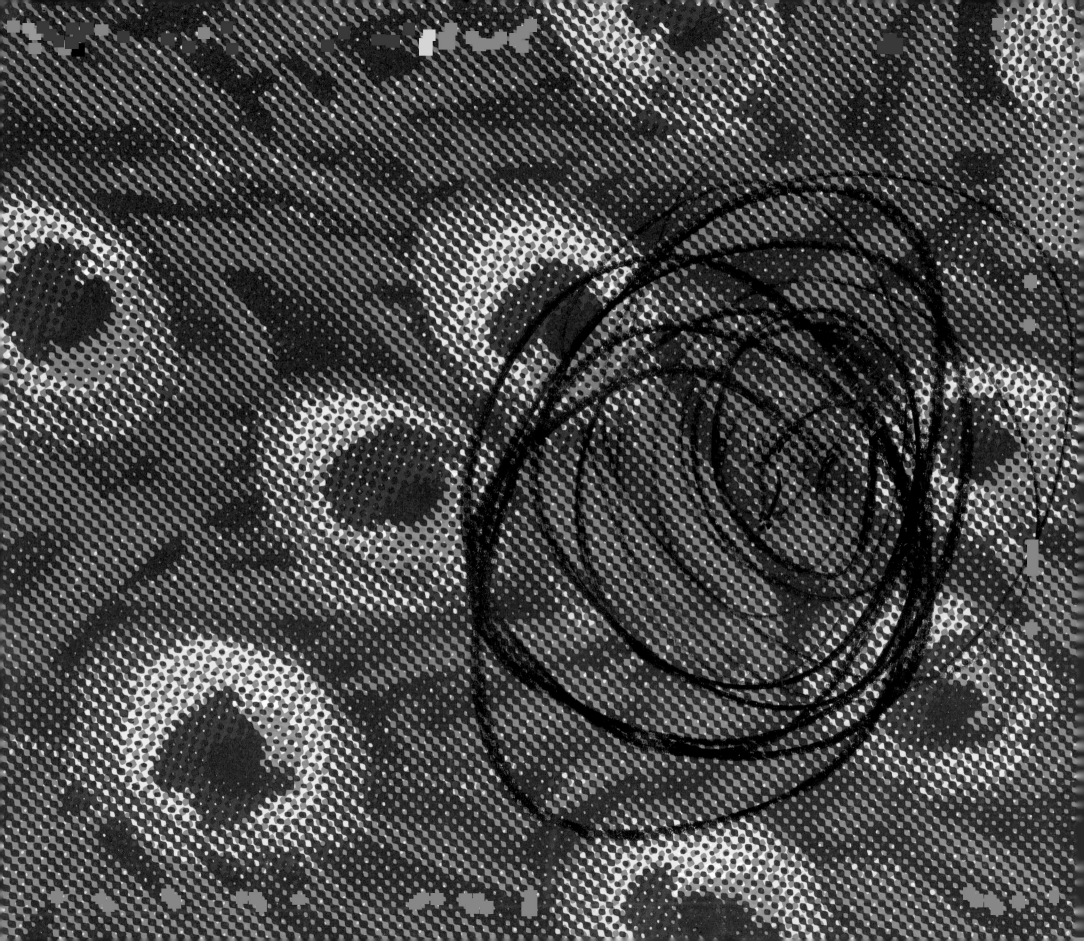